A TEACHER'S LIFE

Colm Cuffe

Gill Books

For Carol and Cian

JUST A REGULAR START TO A TEACHER'S DAY.

GOOOOD MORNING EVERYONE !!!

TEEEACHER...

WHEN'S IT HOMETIME?

JUST
IN CASE
THE
TEACHER
DIDN'T
KNOW.

THE ONE THING YOU DON'T LEARN
IN TEACHER TRAINING COLLEGE...

HOW TO FIX A PHOTOCOPIER.

CURIOSITY IS THE KEY TO
LEARNING, AND QUESTIONS
ARE ONE OF THE MOST
POWERFUL TOOLS FOR
ALLOWING A CHILD TO
THINK INDEPENDENTLY.
WHEN A CHILD ASKS A
QUESTION THEY ARE TAKING
AN ACTIVE ROLE IN THEIR
OWN LEARNING. AS THEY
ASK QUESTIONS,
THEY ARE
DEVELOPING
CRITICAL
THINKING SKILLS
THAT BUILD
BRAIN POWER:

TEEEEACHER?

YES, MARK?

IS 'SCALLYWAG' A BAD WORD?

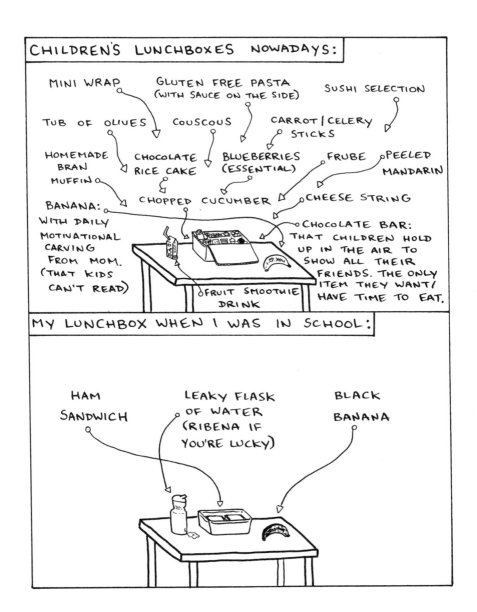

A
TEACHER
MAY NOT
BE A
DENTIST
BUT...

A
CHILD
THINKS
SO.

TEACHER!
TEACHER!
TEACHER!
TEACHER!

TEACHER!
TEACHER!!
TEACHER!

TEACHER!
TEACHER!
TEACHER!!
TEACHER!

WHAT IS IT?

RYAN'S EATING **CHOCOLATE** FOR LUNCH...

AND IT'S NOT TREAT DAY!

IF A TEACHER GOT A CENT FOR EVERY TIME THEY HEARD THIS...

LIFE CYCLE
OF A
SCHOOLYARD
JOKE:

HEY LIAM!
WHAT'S YOUR
FAVOURITE
COLOUR!?

UM, I DUNNO
... BLUE.

SPELL
IT!

B-L-U...
NO!
I SAID SPELL
'IT'... 'I-T'.

BWA HA HA
HA HA HA
HA HA HA
HA HA HA!!

HEY ELLA!
WHAT'S YOUR
FAVOURITE
COLOUR!?

PINK!

SPELL
IT!

P-I-N...
NO!
I SAID SPELL
'IT'... 'I-T'.

MWA HA HA
HA HA HA
HA HA HA!!

HEY RYAN!
WHAT'S YOUR
FAVOURITE
COLOUR!?

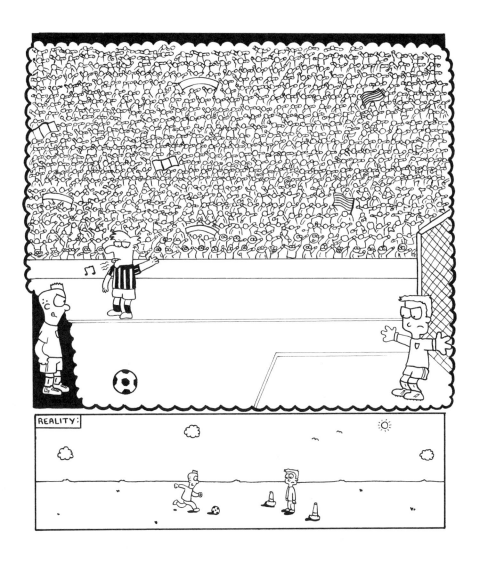

| THIS WILL HAPPEN TO EVERY TEACHER IN THEIR CAREER. | ALAS, THEY MUST FACE THEIR FEAR. | TYING A WET SHOELACE... | ON A DRY DAY. |

THE WORST
POSSIBLE SITUATION
IN A STAFFROOM

OH MY GOD!
NOBODY PANIC ... BUT,
WE'RE OUTTA MILK!

THE ONE DAY TEACHER DOESN'T SHAVE:

TEACHER!?

SOPHIE CALLED ME UGLY.

NO I DIDN'T!

HE'S TELLING PORKY PIES.

SHE DID! SHE CALLED ME UGLY.

NO I DIDN'T!

HEY GUYS!! DID I CALL LIAM UGLY!!?

THINK I'LL GO FOR A WALK.

GHUAHH!

OH NO!

SLAM!

A FULL MOON... EVERY TEACHER'S BIGGEST FEAR.

WHOOSH!

THE MOMENT YOU REALISE YOU'VE BEEN TEACHING INFANTS FOR TOO LONG.

HI, COULD I GET A QUOTATION, PLEASE?

NO PROBLEM, SIR, AND WHEN IS YOUR CAR INSURANCE UP FOR RENEWAL?

THREE MORE SLEEPS.

DAY BEFORE
MID-TERM
BREAK:

FIRST
DAY
BACK:

JUST A REGULAR START TO A TEACHER'S DAY.

TEACHER !?

ON THURSDAY IT'S GONNA BE MY BROTHER'S BIRTHDAY AND HE'S GONNA HAVE A PARTY!

AND WE'RE GONNA GET A BOUNCING CASTLE!

AND WE'RE GONNA GET A CAKE!

AND IT'S GONNA BE THIIIIIIIS BIG!

AND HE'S GONNA GET PRESENTS.

AND I'M ALLOWED GET A PRESENT TOO, EVEN THOUGH IT'S NOT MY BIRTHDAY!

FRIDAY MORNING:

SO... SOPHIE, HOW WAS THE PARTY YESTERDAY?

WHAT PARTY?

A
TEACHER
MAY NOT
BE A
DOCTOR
BUT...

THIS
WORKS
EVERY
TIME.

CLASSROOM DOMINO EFFECT...

ZIPS...

STUDENT TEACHERS...

YOU'VE BEEN WARNED.

JUST A REGULAR START TO A TEACHER'S DAY.

CALENDARS DURING THE SCHOOL TERM:

ESSENTIAL.

CALENDARS DURING THE HOLIDAYS:

OPTIONAL.

BACK TO SCHOOL AFTER THE HOLIDAYS...

GUARANTEED FULL ATTENDANCE.

JUST A REGULAR START TO A TEACHER'S DAY.

GOOOOD MORNING EVERYONE!!!

TEEEACHER...

I FORGOT MY SCHOOL BAG.

SCHOOL TOUR SEASON:

WHICH MEANS COUNTING... LOTS AND LOTS OF COUNTING.

WHY ARE
YOU
COVERING
YOUR EYES,
ADAM?

IF I
LOOK...

THEN I'LL
HAVE TO
WRITE
ABOUT IT.

THAT EVENING:

TEACHERS IN SEPTEMBER.

TEACHERS IN JUNE.

TEACHERS IN SCHOOL...

SO, DOES ANYONE KNOW WHAT DAY IT IS TODAY?

HMMM...

TEACHERS ON THEIR SUMMER HOLIDAYS...

WHAT DAY IS IT TODAY?

BEFORE
SUMMER
HOLIDAYS:

LESSON
PLANNING

MOMENT
OF
SUMMER
HOLIDAYS:

WOO
HOO!

DURING
SUMMER
HOLIDAYS:

TEACHER
SUMMER COURSE

BACK TO SCHOOL COUNTDOWN FOR TEACHERS ON THEIR SUMMER HOLIDAYS.	A VISUAL GUIDE:	14 DAYS LEFT:  BLISS	13 DAYS LEFT:  RELAXATION

12 DAYS LEFT:  CONTENTMENT	11 DAYS LEFT:  SUDDEN AWARENESS OF IMPENDING ROUTINE	10 DAYS LEFT:  RESENTMENT	9 DAYS LEFT:  PURE GRUMPINESS

8 DAYS LEFT:  SPLITTING HEADACHE	7 DAYS LEFT:  FLEETING PANIC ATTACK	6 DAYS LEFT:  DESPERATION	5 DAYS LEFT:  ANXIETY

4 DAYS LEFT:  DESPAIR	3 DAYS LEFT:  DENIAL	2 DAYS LEFT:  SUDDEN URGE TO BOOK A FLIGHT	1 DAY LEFT:  THE FEAR

HOW WAS YOUR SUMMER, LIAM?

BORING.

MY, HOW THE HOLIDAYS GO SO FAST.

Gill Books
Hume Avenue
Park West
Dublin 12
www.gillbooks.ie

Gill Books is an imprint of M.H. Gill and Co.

978 07171 8086 8

Printed by BZ Graf, Poland

The paper used in this book comes from the wood pulp
of managed forests. For every tree felled, at least one
tree is planted, thereby renewing natural resources.

A CIP catalogue record for this book is available from
the British Library.

5 4 3 2 1